Dudley Baptist Church

Presented to

Simeon Fisher

Dated

20 - 7 - 2014

Signed

Elsie Brayne

Seek the Lord,

Isaiah ch. 55 v. 6

A journey back to the cross

The Magnificent Amazing Time Machine

Sinclair B. Ferguson

10 9 8 7 6 5 4 3 2 1
© Copyright 2011 Sinclair B. Ferguson

ISBN: 978-1-84550-547-9
Published by Christian Focus Publications,
Geanies House, Fearn, Tain, Ross-shire,
IV20 1TW, Scotland, U.K.

Cover design by Daniel van Straaten
Illustrations by Ed Olson
Printed in China

A journey back to the cross

The Magnificent Amazing Time Machine

Sinclair B. Ferguson

Illustrated by Ed Olson

CF4·K

Hi there! Let's go on a journey in an amazing time machine. It can travel backwards through the centuries. I wonder where we will go? Now it would be scary to go on your own, so it's a good job this time machine can take passengers! Get on board and come with me. Are you ready to travel in time — back to the very beginning? Whoosh! We're on our way!

Hey! Look at this! We're in the 1960s. There's a spaceship going to the moon! And now it's the nineteenth century. I saw Queen Victoria.

That's an American soldier fighting for independence in 1776. And there's Robert the Bruce at the Battle of Bannockburn in 1314.

Look over there—that city is on fire! It's Rome! The Sack of Rome took place in 410 A.D. Now we've reached the first century. I've just seen the apostle Paul in prison. What's Peter doing outside that empty tomb? Is that a cross in the distance?

And there's David. See—Goliath's lying on the ground!

It must be Adam and Eve. God is sending them away because of their sin. They won't be able to live in the garden that God made for them. How terrible!

'After Adam and Eve turn against us, we must save people from the terrible results of their sin. Here is the plan.'

Who's he speaking to?
Can you hear another voice?

'Father, I am willing to die in order to save men and women and boys and girls.'

That must be God the Son speaking! But there is a third voice.

'We are agreed—I, God the Holy Spirit, will help people to understand what the Son will do, and how they can be saved from the terrible results of sin. The Plan will work!'

What is this plan they are talking about? Did that plan succeed? Look at this! Pictures are appearing on the time screen. Perhaps this will show us what happened...

It looks as if we're going on another journey through time. But it's forwards this time.

Noah has just come out of the ark, with the animals. God has promised not to flood the world again.

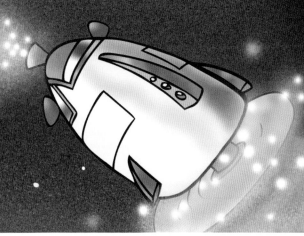

I've just spotted Abraham. He is looking up at the stars. God has just promised that the Saviour will come from his family.

Let's see what happens next.

'We will show the people what you will do, my Son. Daily sacrifices will remind them of their sin. Once a year the High Priest will make a sacrifice, but you will be the Great Sacrifice! The other sacrifices are only pictures to show the people what you will do.'

There go Mary and Joseph on the road to Bethlehem—just the two of them. See, over there—men riding camels! They are looking up at a star in the night sky.

Listen to the Father again: 'A star will announce your birth. Those who have never heard about you will learn that you have come to be their Saviour.'
The Son says, 'I will go, Father.'
'They cannot be saved unless you die for them on the Cross. Are you willing to die for them?'
'Yes, Father I am!'
'The plan will work.'

Jesus died for our sins and the Father raised him to new life!

There's Peter preaching in Jerusalem on the Day of Pentecost. The Holy Spirit has come and many people from all over the world have trusted in Jesus.

Now what's this on the screen? It's a map of the world. Those arrows point to all the places where people have heard about God's plan.

And look, that arrow is pointing at your town and that's your street. There is an arrow pointing at your church. Hold on tight, we're slowing down. We're home!

I feel as if I have travelled for ever, don't you?
What a wonderful adventure we've been on.
We've got loads of stories to tell.
God's plan really did succeed!

Just in case you need a bit of help — here are some words that you can use to tell others about God's plan. They are from the Gospel according to John.

God so loved the world that he gave his only Son so that whoever believes in him should not perish but have everlasting life. John 3: 16

That is the Plan. That is the message Jesus wants you to tell others.

Will you?

CF4K

Are you looking for children's books that you can rely on? Do you want your children to know the truth about Jesus Christ? Well Christian Focus Publications have the right books for you. CF4K has a strong list of tried and tested titles that take God's Word and apply it to real life - to a child's life. CF4K publishes books that show how Jesus is the way, the only way to know God.

For church, for home, CF4K supplies everything you and your family need to learn about God, salvation and the good news of Jesus Christ. From pre-school to teenage fiction, we have it covered!

Find us at our web page:
www.christianfocus.com